PRAISE POEMS

INSPIRED BY GOD THROUGH PSALMS

BY MILEY WHITE

iUniverse, Inc.
Bloomington

Praise Poems
Inspired by God Through Psalms

iUniverse books may be ordered through booksellers or by contacting:

iUniverse
1663 Liberty Drive
Bloomington, IN 47403
www.iuniverse.com
1-800-Authors (1-800-288-4677)

ISBN: 978-1-4502-8657-2 (pbk)
ISBN: 978-1-4502-8658-9 (ebk)

Printed in the United States of America

iUniverse rev. date: 1/15/2011

This is for YOU.

You are fearfully and wonderfully made.

Contents

Preface   xiii

Book 1   1

1.	Meditate	2
2.	Son	3
3.	Rise	4
4.	Search	5
5.	Morning Prayer	6
6.	Heal	7
7.	Save	8
8.	Feet	9
9.	Endure	10
10.	Wicked	11
11.	Every	12
12.	Say	13
13.	Come	14
14.	Turn	15
15.	Good	16
16.	Saints	17
17.	Protection	18
18.	Rescued	19
19.	God	20
20.	Defense	21
21.	Power	22
22.	Aid	23
23.	Keeper	24
24.	Pure	25
25.	Path	26
26.	Integrity	27
27.	Light	28

28.	Honor	29
29.	Voice	30
30.	Thanks	31
31.	You	32
32.	Need	33
33.	Lord	34
34.	Right	35
35.	Chase	36
36.	Preserves	37
37.	Cursed	38
38.	Angry	39
39.	Anguish	40
40.	Rejoice	41
41.	Sick	42
	Revelations	43

Book 2   45

42.	Thirsts	46
43.	Plead	47
44.	Abandoned	48
45.	Groom	49
46.	Moving	50
47.	Inheritance	51
48.	Great	52
49.	Wealth	53
50.	Actions	54
51.	Grace	55
52.	Tongue	56
53.	Foolish	57
54.	Helper	58
55.	End	59
56.	Army	60
57.	Soul	61
58.	Serve	62
59.	Strength	63

60.	Battles	64
61.	Nowhere	65
62.	Nothing	66
63.	Communication	67
64.	Words	68
65.	Provide	69
66.	Flood	70
67.	Praise	71
68.	Flee	72
69.	Suffering	73
70.	Bow	74
71.	Old	75
72.	King	76
	Reflections	77

Book 3   79

73.	Trappings	80
74.	Enemies	81
75.	Works	82
76.	Heard	83
77.	Stay	84
78.	Hope	85
79.	Heathens	86
80.	Smile	87
81.	Listen	88
82.	Judges	89
83.	Israel	90
84.	Yearns	91
85.	Revive	92
86.	Call	93
87.	Zion	94
88.	Grave	95
89.	Reassurance	96
	Review	97

Book 4   99

90.	Existence	100
91.	Trust	101
92.	Mesmerizing	102
93.	Strong	103
94.	Punish	104
95.	Worship	105
96.	Give	106
97.	Fierce	107
98.	Salvation	108
99.	Reigns	109
100.	His	110
101.	Wise	111
102.	Attend	112
103.	Bless	113
104.	Look	114
105.	Appointed	115
106.	Ourselves	116
	Releases	117

Book 5   119

107.	Wonder	120
108.	Glory	121
109.	Fall	122
110.	Sit	123
111.	Seek	124
112.	Delight	125
113.	Uplifting	126
114.	Sea	127
115.	Reward	128
116.	Mercy	129
117.	People	130
118.	Confidence	131
119.	Doubt	132

120. Distress   133
121. Preserves   134
122. Abode   135
123. Scorn   136
124. Waters   137
125. Anchor   138
126. Captivity   139
127. Rely   140
128. Follow   141
129. Stand   142
130. Forgiveness   143
131. Behave   144
132. Commit   145
133. Anointed   146
134. House   147
135. Name   148
136. Goodness   149
137. Worth   150
138. Trouble   151
139. Eyes   152
140. Dwell   153
141. Guard   154
142. Overwhelmed   155
143. Justified   156
144. Humbled   157
145. Generation   158
146. Sing   159
147. Heart   160
148. Universal   161
149. Kingdom   162
150. Breath   163
     Rewinds   164

Afterward   165

Preface

Relationships between God and man are powerful and passionate. In dealing with these situations, each of these poems has a message that should be used as a quick reference when time is limited or along beside the original Psalm when deeper meanings are sought. The number preceding each poem represents the chapter from which that poem originated. A brief summary of ten points gathered follow each book. The style is simple and the subjects are varied with focus on the positive perspective.

Have you ever read the book of Psalms? It is centrally located within the Bible and one of the most often read works. Every emotion is addressed. God was the motivator and author through his servants back in the days of King David. This author simply took what was done then and put a modern day spin on it, condensing each chapter into poetry followed by a single reflective verse taken from the King James Bible.

The concept for this book is the result of my answered prayer for guidance. I sincerely asked God what I could do to contribute to His kingdom. The answer was to write these poems. Allow me a few moments to share my experience with you so you can better understand how this work came into existence.

My remembrance of the relationship between God and myself started when I was a child (5 years old). While playing one day with my younger brother and older sisters, I experienced a life changing event. We were all playing in the yard at the home where we grew up. Being fascinated (as children are) to our daddy's car, we all ended up getting into it. Little did I know then, that was not the only thing I was getting into!

Originally, the car was parked in the path just above a steep hill. One of us (I still do not know who or if it was just an accident) put the car in gear and it started to roll, headed towards a tree. We all began screaming as it increased in speed. I had never been so terrified in my entire life! All those church sermons I had heard finally caught up with me. I knew about God but had not accepted him into my heart. I was a mean little girl and if I was to die at that moment, I was sure I was headed for Hell. Looking back, I can now see that the car was actually rolling into my future.

I prayed that if God would get us out of this alive I would dedicate my life to Him. I still do not know who was brave and smart enough to hit the brakes just before the car crashed into the tree. I only know I was very traumatized and shaking with nervousness. My parents and grandmother came running to help get us out of the vehicle. They could see that I was physically unharmed as I ran away from them and towards the house. In my room I remembered my promise. Now that God had delivered me from that scene, it was my turn to keep my word to Him.

I faced myself in the mirror and vowed with determination that from that time forward I would do my best to live so that when the time came for me to leave this life, I would be assured of another home waiting (heaven) and my host (God) would greet me with a smile. What a scary, yet exciting time that was for me!

I had a lot of life to live and I needed to live it with the knowledge that God was watching my every move.

Accepting God was the first step in getting to know Him. From that day forward, I have grown and learned so much (but never enough) about God, his Son and his Son's gifts to us. As I grew taller and smarter I saw that the danger with the car was not as great as I had thought it to be at the time. The hill no longer looked so steep or the distance so far as it did then. God did not start watching me that day; He had known me all along. Through the years I have not always lived the way we are instructed through Bible teachings. Whenever I venture away, I am drawn again to Him and placed back on the right path. Not only have I accepted God but I discovered that He has accepted me.

Now (fifty years later) my thoughts wander as I look back and ask myself "what will I be remembered for once this life ends?" Nothing great comes to mind. As I look ahead I ask "how I can contribute to the future?" As I look up I pray "Lord, what can I do for your kingdom while I am still here?" There are so many wonderful causes God's people have dedicated themselves to working with, ranging from educating children to helping out the elderly. I want a ministry also. My heavenly Father knew even before I asked. He was simply waiting for me to seek Him.

The answer came immediately when I looked up. The answer to my prayer filled me with wonder and delight. It was customized for me and here are the thoughts that helped me get to where I am today. "Our future is to praise God. Why wait until we are with Him to praise him? Why not start praising Him now? How? What format will my praise take? I am a quiet person with a big spirit. I must express myself without yelling. I do not have a voice for singing. I do love writing. I love poems!! I could write praise poems! Where do I get praise poems? Where do praises come from? Praises come from God, from God's people, from

God's word, from the Bible. Where in the Bible? Psalms is full of praises! They have already been written. Rewrite them so people in our fast paced world today can understand and appreciate their meanings. Keep them simple and short. Bring a new flavor to an old standard." Thanksgiving and praises to God were my response. The verse that came to mind was from Matthew 7:7 Ask, and it shall be given you; seek, and you shall find; knock, and it shall be opened unto you.

God gave me the words of poetry through Psalms. I could not wait to begin the project! I would write every spare moment I got after work in the evenings, on weekends and even early morning hours before the sun rose. It was a work I delighted in performing. I was using my time of mediation with Him to write these words for you. When the words flowed I could not seem to write fast enough. After each book, I wrote ten summary points I believed to be the key things that were taken from that book. Sometimes I would get to or return to a section that took a while. I prayed and God helped me come up with the best words for each poem. My wish is that you be as inspired reading them as I was writing them. These simple yet powerful poems are another one of God's blessings to us. They can help enrich the time spent in His presence.

Book 1

Meditate

Meditate day and night.
In God's laws, find delight!
Bad decisions are swept away.
Success, love and peace remain.

Psalms1:1 Happy is the person that delights
in the law of the Lord.

Son

This day I will proclaim,
You are my son, my same.
Ask me and I will give,
Blessings to all who trust him!

Psalms 2:11 Serve the Lord with fear,
and rejoice with trembling.

Rise

Many rise up against me.
You smite them on the cheek.
I cried to you with a loud voice.
You heard and now I rejoice.

Psalms 3:6 I will not be afraid of
ten thousands of people ...

Search

Search your heart before you fall asleep.
Gladness is more than food to eat.
Money will not give lasting peace.
Only the Lord can keep you in safety.

Psalm 4:3 … the Lord has set apart
him that is godly for himself.

Morning Prayer

My morning prayer to you I call.
Let the rebellious transgressor fall.
Those that trust in God rejoice.
Your defense is in the Lord!

Psalm 5:8 Lead me, O Lord…

Heal

Lord please, have mercy on me.
Heal me. I am weak.
Deliver my soul from grief.
Bring shame upon my enemies.

Psalm 6:9 The Lord hath heard my supplication;
the Lord will receive my prayer.

Save

I trust you God to save me!
I am being chased by my enemy.
Judge him for doing wrong.
I never did him any harm.

Psalm 7:11 God judgeth the righteous, and
God is angry with the wicked every day.

Feet

You created the moon and the stars.
Beasts, fish and fowl are all yours.
Why would you cater to mans needs?
You put it all under our feet!

Psalm 8:9 ... how excellent is
thy name in all the earth!

Endure

The Lord shall endure forever.
He is a refuge in times of trouble.
To the needy He brings salvation.
Humans forget that men form nations.

Psalm 9:16 The Lord is known by the
judgement which he executeth.

Wicked

The wicked is full of pride and vanity.
They seek to prey upon the poor in humanity.
The wicked has a cursing tongue
and deceitful heart.
Evil will perish, when God takes part.

Psalm 10:16 The Lord is king forever and ever:
the heathen are perished out of his land.

Every

God sees our every move!
Do you think he approves?
He hates those that hurt others.
He sees the good and serves justice.

Psalm 11:4 ... the Lord's throne is in heaven: his eyes behold, his eyelids try, the children of men.

Say

Hear me Lord as I pray.
Deliver us from what we say.
Some verbs sound vain or untrue.
Only pure words come from you.

Psalm 12:3 The Lord shall cut off all flattering
lips and the tongue that speaketh proud things.

Come

I need you to hear my plea Lord.
My enemies sneer thinking they have won.
How much longer God before you come?
In your love I will always trust.

Psalm: 13:3 Consider and hear me, O
Lord my God: lighten mine eyes …

Turn

Humans are lost in corruption!
The race is in need of reconstruction.
Everyone, turn once again to God.
True joy comes from the Lord.

Psalm 14:2 The Lord looked down from heaven
upon the children of men to see if there were
any that did understand and seek God.

Good

Who will live with the Lord?
One must be true to his word!
He is good to his neighbor.
He will not be bought with favors.

Psalm 15:1 Lord who shall abide in thy tabernacle?

Saints

I expect my reward.
It comes from the Lord
When saints on earth pass
They come to God at last.

Psalm 16:5 The Lord is the portion of
mine inheritance and of my cup...

Protection

My enemies seek to devour me!
They are like a lion that is greedy.
From them come evil accusations.
I pray God, for your protection.

Psalm 17:6 I have called upon thee
for thou wilt hear me, O God…

Rescued

I was surrounded by enemies!
There was a sea of ungodly men!
God heard my distressed cry.
You rescued your servant's life!

Psalm 18:50 Great deliverance giveth he
to his king; and showeth mercy to his
anointed, to David, and to his seed

God

The heavens above proclaim,
God has wisdom. God has fame.
His laws are pure and right.
Obey them and be enlightened.

Psalm 19:8 The statues of the Lord
are right, rejoicing the heart…

Defense

Our king was troubled and tense.
God came to your defense.
We now rejoice in your salvation.
You serve the God of creation.

Psalm 20:1 The Lord hear thee in the day of trouble; the name of the God of Jacob defend thee

Power

God answered his servant's prayer.
He gave him honor and health.
Our Lord has the strength and power.
He can bless good or burn evil out!

Psalm 21:1 The King shall joy
in thy strength, O Lord;

Aid

You are my God from birth.
It is in you I trust.
Come now to my aid.
Forever your name deserves praise.

Psalm 22:22 I will declare thy
name unto my brethren...

Keeper

The Lord is my keeper.
I will fear no evil.
He pours oil on my head.
Into his house I am lead.

Psalm 23:4 Yea, though I walk through
the valley… I will fear no evil…

Pure

You must have clean hands!
The one with a pure heart can enter in.
Come to the holy place, climb the hill!
The temple is where our Lord will live.

Psalm 24:1 The earth is the Lord's, and the fullness
thereof; the world, and they that dwell therein.

Path

There is a path of truth and grace.
I need you to show me the way.
Please forgive my transgressions.
Remove from me my oppressions.

Psalm 25:1 Unto thee, O Lord,
do I lift up my soul.

Integrity

Bless the Lord, trust in God.
Walk in truth, honor His word!
Examine me and you will see.
I live my life with integrity.

Psalm 26:11 But as for me, I will walk in mine integrity: redeem me, and be merciful unto me.

Light

I refuse to fear.
My enemy aims his spear.
God is my light.
He preserves my life.

Psalm 27:1 The Lord is my light and
my salvation, whom shall I fear?

Honor

We started out the same.
They did not honor your name.
Now they want to destroy me.
Save us Lord! Send us peace!

Psalm 28:1 Unto thee will I cry, O Lord my rock…

Voice

I hear the voice of the Lord!
It is present in the storm.
God has earth shaking power!
Give Him glory forever.

Psalm 29:3 The voice of the Lord is upon
the waters: the God of glory thundereth:

Thanks

Lord you lifted me up.
You kept my soul from dust!
To you I give thanks.
Praise Him saints!

Psalm 30:11 Thou hast turned for me
my mourning into dancing...

You

There are liars, slanderers and vain men.
They counsel together to plan my end.
In your presence Lord I hide
You are my rock, you are my guide.

Psalm 31:24 Be of good courage, and he shall
strengthen your heart, all ye that hope in the Lord.

Need

I have to confess.
Against you I transgress.
God, I need your forgiveness.
Send your guidance and deliverance.

Psalm 32:1 Blessed is he whose transgression
is forgiven, whose sin is covered.

Lord

In our Lord we rejoice!
Sing to him in a loud voice.
The earth is full of his creations.
His love extends to all generations.

Psalm 33:14 From the place of his habitation he
looketh upon all the inhabitants of the earth

Right

Do the right thing in the Lord's eyes.
His ears are open to your cries.
The angel of the Lord is near!
He will deliver you from fear.

Psalm 34:22 The Lord redeemeth the
soul of his servants: and none of them
that trust in him shall be desolate.

Chase

Lord, send them confusion and shame.
The evil ones wish me pain.
Let your angel chase them off.
Their persecution of me is false.

Psalm 35:26 Let them be ashamed and brought
to confusion together that rejoice at mine hurt:

Preserves

Evil men have no fear of God.
In selfish plots, they are lost.
My Lord preserves man and beast.
He invites the righteous to his feast.

Psalm 36:7 How excellent is thy loving kindness,
O God! Therefore the children of men put
their trust under the shadow of thy wings.

Cursed

Evil doers seek to destroy.
They target the just, the needy and the poor.
Cruel men are cursed and will soon be cut down.
When you search, they are nowhere to be found.

Psalm 37:29 The righteous shall inherit
the land, and dwell therein forever.

Angry

You are angry with me!
You hate my immorality.
I need you. I am weak.
Please do not forsake me.

Psalm 38:21 Foresake me not, O Lord:
O my God, be not far from me.

Anguish

Self control was not the key!
I suffered it all, and did not speak.
Words of anguish burst from me!
"Spare me Lord!" is my plea.

Psalm 39:7 And now, Lord, what
wait I for? My hope is in thee.

Rejoice

The Lord heard my cry and delivered me!
I rejoice upon the rock where he put my feet.
I will declare God's loyalty and salvation.
He has plans for everyone in the congregation.

Psalm 40:2 He brought me up also
out of a horrible pit, out of the miry
clay, and set my feet upon a rock,

Sick

I was sick and in bed.
My enemy wished me dead.
Even my friend turned away.
Lord, you were the only one who stayed.

Psalm 41:4 I said, Lord, be merciful unto me:
heal my soul; for I have sinned against thee.

Revelations

1. King David called upon God for help.
2. God heard David's prayers.
3. God answered David's prayers.
4. David praised God for helping him.
5. Helping David fight battles meant God destroying his own creations.
6. God prefers praise over sacrifice.
7. God was angry with David's transgressions.
8. David acknowledged sin and begged forgiveness.
9. God preserved and forgave King David.
10. God is merciful. He made David a forefather of Jesus.

Book 2

Thirsts

My soul thirsts for God.
He is the living word.
Lord, continue my song.
Do not let me be forgotten.

Psalm 42:9 I will say unto God my
rock, why hast thou forgotten me?

Plead

O God, plead my case!
Extend to me your grace.
In you I place my hope.
Deliver me, uplift my soul.

Psalm 43:5 Why art thou cast down, o
my soul? And why art thou disquieted
within me? Hope in God:

Abandoned

This nation feels abandoned by God.
We still boast of him all day long.
You no longer battle for us as in days past.
God, we need your strength to last!

Psalm 44:23 Awake, why sleepest thou, O
Lord? Arise, cast us not off for ever.

Groom

It is a glorious sight to see.
Here is a meek and mighty groom to be.
He is robed in pleasant smelling garments.
Rejoice in those rich unrevealed presents!

Psalm 45:15 With gladness and rejoicing shall they
be brought: they shall enter into the king's palace.

Moving

The mountains are carried into the sea.
The earth melts and wars cease.
Do no be afraid, do not fear.
Our God is moving all around here.

Psalm 46:1 God is our refuge and strength,
a very present help in trouble.

Inheritance

Clap your hands and sing praises to God.
We have a great inheritance.
Our God is king of all the earth.
We exist in his universe.

Psalm 47:7 For God is the king of all the
earth; sing ye praises with understanding.

Great

Great is the Lord our God!
He delivered the city from trouble.
Praise Him forever and ever.
Rejoice and tell it to generations hereafter.

Psalm 48:14 For this God is our God for ever
and ever: he will be our guide even unto death.

Wealth

Do not put your trust in riches.
Wise men die, fools and brutes perish.
Wealth can not redeem souls.
It is to God we must hold.

Psalm 49:15 But God will redeem my soul from
the power of the grave: for he shall receive me.

Actions

God will judge his people.
Watch your actions and what you speak of.
Give offerings with praise and thanksgiving.
Forget God and risk being torn to ribbons.

Psalm 50:23 Whoso offereth praise glorifieth
me: and to him that ordereth his conversation
aright will I show the salvation of God.

Grace

I have sinned and come short.
Lord, restore your joy to my heart.
Forgive, have mercy, this I pray.
Cleanse, deliver and give me your grace.

Psalm 51:2 Wash me thoroughly from mine
iniquity, and cleanse me from my sin.

Tongue

The lying tongue cuts deep!
It is full of mischief and deceit.
Boasting will get you killed.
God's people continue to prosper and live.

Psalms 52:7 Lo. This is the man that
made not God his strength; but trusted
in the abundance of his riches ...

Foolish

The foolish man does his own thing.
He is unaware and unbelieving.
Our creator looks down from heaven.
He is not pleased with man's misunderstanding.

Psalm 53:2 God looked down from heaven
upon the children of men, to see if there were
any that did understand, that did seek God.

Helper

The Lord is my helper.
He sees the oppressors.
He will save and deliver me
I praise his name freely.

Psalm 54:2 Hear my prayer, O God;
give ear to the words of my mouth.

End

I thought he was my friend.
I found out in the end.
He is a wicked enemy.
He seeks to destroy me.

Psalm 55:21 The words of his mouth
were smoother than butter, but war was
in his heart; his words were softer than
oil, yet they were drawn swords.

Army

An army of enemies are here to fight.
Have mercy, O thou Most High!
In you I trust, I will not fear.
My preserver, it is you I revere.

Psalms 56:11 In God have I put my trust: I
will not be afraid what man can do unto me.

Soul

My soul trusts in God!
He will protect me from their sword.
Into their own pit, the enemy falls.
Give glory to God who sees all.

Psalm 57:2 I will cry unto God most high;
unto God that performeth all things for me.

Serve

It started from their time of youth.
The wicked departed from the truth.
Break them, melt them, and blow them away.
Serve justice to reward your good people's loyalty.

Psalm 58:10 The righteous shall rejoice
when he seeth the vengeance:

Strength

Deliver me from their lying tongues!
Bloodthirsty men seek the innocent.
Trap and consume them. Give me strength!
You are my God, my refuge and my defense.

Psalm 59:1 Deliver me from mine enemies, O my
God: defend me from them that rise up against me.

Battles

All around us battles abound.
Armies are aiming to take us down.
You, our God are what we need.
Deliver us from our enemies.

Psalm 60:11 Give us help from trouble
for vain is the help of man.

Nowhere

What other name do I know?
There is nowhere else to go!
I reach to you my God.
You are my shelter, tower, and rock.

Psalm 61:2 From the end of the earth will I
cry unto thee, when my heart is overwhelmed.
Lead me to the rock that is higher than I.

Nothing

Man is full of mischief.
He trusts in his riches.
We are really nothing without God!
He is the one to whom all power belongs.

Psalm 62:5 My soul, wait thou only upon
God; for my expectation is from him.

Communication

God, you are my foundation.
With you, I need communication.
There is no other hope that I know.
Only you can save my soul.

Psalm 63:8 My soul followeth hard after
thee: thy right hand upholdeth me.

Words

Bitter words come from wicked tongues.
They secretly plot to do wrongs.
Trust God who hears and sees all.
On their own words they shall fall!

Psalm 64:8 So they shall make their own
tongue to fall upon themselves: …

Provide

In God's presence people, abide.
Trust Him, to provide.
He waters the earth with rain.
Our prayers are answered in amazing ways.

Psalm 65:2 O thou that hearest prayer,
unto thee shall all flesh come.

Flood

Sing praises to our awesome God.
He brought us through a flood!
He has done wonders for this land.
Before him with our offerings we stand.

Psalm 66:1 Make a joyful noise
unto God, all ye lands:

Praise

Praise God everyone for his mercy!
He will judge nations righteously.
Be glad and sing for joy.
Our earth has much in store!

Psalm 67:4 O let the nations be glad and
sing for joy: for thou shalt judge the people
righteously, and govern the nations upon earth.

Flee

Wicked flee from God's presence!
He will not tolerate their pretense.
True worshippers only, he will welcome.
They will protect and strengthen his kingdom.

Psalm 68:8 The earth shook, the heavens
also dropped at the presence of God ...

Suffering

On you Lord, I will wait.
I suffer the shame and the hate.
Deliver me, redeem my soul.
We sing thanks to our God of hosts.

Psalm 69:6 Let not them that wait on thee, O
Lord God of hosts, be ashamed for my sake: let not
those that seek thee be confounded for my sake,

Bow

Help me Lord, I need you now.
It is before you I bow.
Shame and confuse my foes.
Come quickly to save my soul.

Psalm 70:5 But I am poor and needy:
make haste unto me, O God: thou
art my help and my deliverer;

Old

Lord, I need you when I am old and gray.
Then more than ever, I need you to stay.
Confound and consume my adversaries.
Help me show others your power and mercy.

Psalm 71:18 Now also, when I am old and
gray headed, O God, forsake me not;

King

When the king comes, we will see.
A new day dawns of prosperity and peace.
The poor are precious in his sight
Nations will flourish in his light.

Psalm 72:19 And blessed be his glorious
name forever: and let the whole
earth be filled with this glory.

Amen, and Amen

Reflections

1. The king leads the people.
2. God leads the king.
3. The leader is tortured and tried.
4. There are jealous, greedy enemies who wish the king harm.
5. The king is in constant prayer to His creator seeking peace and strength.
6. David's prayers are answered because his heart is open to God.
7. God destroys the wicked. He confuses them also.
8. David praises God for protecting him and his people with love and mercy.
9. David honors God (builds him a sanctuary) and gives vows to him.
10. The king sees his life as an example for all generations.

Book 3

Trappings

Beware of the trappings of wealth.
Pride and violence affect health.
Life is fleeting and the soul is lost.
Without God, that is the cost.

Psalm 73:26 My flesh and my heart
faileth but God is the strength of my
heart, and my portion forever.

Enemies

Burning the temple cannot destroy.
It still belongs to our Lord.
The world is his to do as he pleases.
Why would you be God's enemy?

Psalm 74:4 Thine enemies roar in the
midst of thy congregations;

Works

The people will be judged.
The rule is according to their works.
There will be a trial in the land.
Your fate is in God's hands.

Psalm 75:7 But God is the judge: he putteth
down one, and setteth up another.

Heard

God is the one!
It is to Him the victory belongs.
His judgments cause fear on earth.
All the way from heaven he is heard.

Psalm 76:11 Vow, and pay unto the Lord your
God: let all that be round about him bring
presents unto him that ought to be feared.

Stay

Please God, stay!
Do not turn away.
Your works are known.
You led them through Moses and Aaron.

Psalm 77:11 I will remember the works of the
Lord: surely I will remember thy wonders of old.

Hope

Set your hope in God.
Stand on his word.
Remember his deeds.
Obey and believe.

Psalm 78:5 For he established a testimony in Jacob, and appointed a law in Israel; which he commanded our fathers, that they should make them known to their children:

Heathens

Great sins were committed!
The heathens did it.
Anger and jealousy from God, it came.
Have mercy Lord, we are not the ones to blame.

Psalm 79:9 Help us, O God of our salvation,
for the glory of thy name: and deliver us, and
purge away our sins, for thy name's sake.

Smile

Lord, we need your smile!
Only you can show us how.
We need to come back together again.
Forgive and renew the son of man.

Psalm 80:3 Turn us again, O God, and cause
thy face to shine; and we shall be saved.

Listen

Listen and you will hear!
Why did I abandon you Israel?
You put other gods before me!
Listen only to me. I am victory!!!

Psalm 81:13 Oh that my people had hearkened
unto me, and Israel had walked in my ways!

Judges

God's judges must be just!
Defend the poor and fatherless.
Serve justice to those afflicted and needy.
Cast off the ones that are wicked and greedy.

Psalm 82:8 Arise, O God, judge the earth:
for thou shalt inherit all nations.

Israel

Israel is why nations congregate.
Against her they gather, to eliminate.
We are your chosen people.
Deliver us from evil!

Psalm 83:4 They have said, come, and let us cut
them off from being a nation; that the name
of Israel may be no more in remembrance.

Yearns

My soul yearns to be near you Lord!
In your temple, I hear your word.
You are my sun and my shield!
In you I trust and place my will.

Psalm 84:10 For a day in thy courts is
better than a thousand. I had rather be a
doorkeeper in the house of my God, than
to dwell in the tents of wickedness.

Revive

Revive us again our Lord.
In you we will rejoice.
Bring your people out of humiliation.
Grant us your mercy and salvation.

Psalms 85:7 Show us thy mercy, O
Lord, and grant us thy salvation.

Call

No other place I know to go.
Only you Lord, can save my soul!
On you I call to give me strength.
Daily I praise you for deliverance.

Psalm 86:12 I will praise thee, O Lord
my God, with all my heart: and I will
glorify thy name for evermore.

Zion

Zion is a lively place to be.
God loves this glorious city.
Recognition is given to its citizens.
Some are singers and musicians.

Psalm 87:2 The Lord loveth the gates of
Zion more than all the dwellings of Jacob

Grave

Deliver me from the grave!
In it there is no praise.
Lord, do not cut me off.
I do not want to be lost.

Psalm 88:14 Lord, why casteth thou off my
soul? Why hidest thou face from me?

Reassurance

Lord, have mercy on your servant.
Remember how you made a covenant?
To David you swore endurance.
Today I need reassurance.

Psalm 89:49 Lord, where are thy
former loving-kindness, which thou
swarest unto David in thy truth?

Review

1. Keep the faith.
2. Hard times must be suffered through.
3. Continue to pray.
4. God is still there.
5. He is setting standards.
6. God has a plan.
7. Be included in God's plans.
8. He loves us. He hears our prayers.
9. God can be jealous or angry.
10. Continue to praise Him anyway.

Book 4

Existence

Your existence my God has been and ever will be.
You were before creations of the
world, the earth, or me.
Moses was here in comparison but a minute.
Give mercy, so new generations can rejoice in it.

Psalm 90:16 Let thy work appear unto thy
servants, and thy glory unto their children.

Trust

Trust in God's presence.
He will be your fortress.
He hides you from the evils of war.
No plagues or snares come with his love.

Psalm 91:11 For he shall give his angels charge
over thee, to keep thee in all thy ways.

Mesmerizing

The thoughts of the Lord are deep.
His works are mesmerizing.
Upright people flourish and grow strong.
Evil flourish then perish for doing wrong.

Psalm 92:13 Those that be planted in the house of
the Lord shall flourish in the courts of our God.

Strong

The Lord is strong.
He rules from his throne.
He can be heard over the flood.
True to good, His laws stood.

Psalms 93:4 The Lord on high is mightier
than the noise of many waters, yea,
than the mighty waves of the sea.

Punish

Do you think you will escape?
Harshly you speak and spirits you break.
God sees and hears your every move!
He will punish evil doers.

Psalm 94:9 He that planted the ear, shall he not
hear? He that formed the eye, shall he not see?

Worship

Worship our God of all gods.
Do not let your hearts be hard.
He created the land and the sea.
Obey and sing praises to our King.

Psalm 95:6 O come, let us worship and bow
down: let us kneel before the Lord our maker.

Give

All day we should praise his name.
Mountains and valleys, God made!
Let the trees sing and the sea shout.
Give due glory to our holy one now!

Psalm 96:4 For the Lord is great, and greatly to
be praised! He is to be feared above all gods.

Fierce

Fierce is our Lord!
Fire and lightings from him soar!
Hills melt at his presence.
He rules in favor of his saints.

Psalm 97:9 For thou, Lord art high above all
the earth: thou art exalted far above all gods.

Salvation

Look to see the Lord's salvation.
Sing and clap with motivation.
He showed his people love and victory.
Rejoice loudly for our judge of equity.

Psalm 98:4 Make a joyful noise unto
the Lord, all the earth: make a loud
noise, and rejoice and sing praise.

Reigns

The Lord reigns over the realm.
He sits between the cherubim.
God judged and punished for wrongs.
Afterward, the forgiveness comes.

Psalm 99:5 Exalt ye the Lord our God, and
worship at his footstool; for he is holy.

His

Nations, gladly serve our Lord.
We are his people and not our own.
Enter into his presence with thanks.
His mercy and truth surpass all ranks.

Psalm 100:5 For the Lord is good;
his mercy is everlasting; and his truth
endureth to all generations.

Wise

Live a wise life.
Stay apart from pride and lies.
Walk with a perfect heart.
In his kingdom, you will be a part.

Psalm 101:6 Mine eyes shall be upon the faithful
of the land, that they may dwell with me:

Attend

I cry to you when I am in trouble.
Lord, attend to me on the double.
My needs are great and my days are short.
You are forever. Do not depart.

Psalm 102:12 But thou, O Lord, shall endure for
ever; and thy remembrance unto all generations.

Bless

Bless the Lord's holy name.
He forgives; he heals and saves from the grave.
He crowns with kindness and mercy.
His hosts and works bless Him
because He is worthy.

Psalm 103:2 Bless the Lord, O my soul,
and forget not all his benefits.

Look

Look everyone, at God's creative work!
He laid the foundations of the earth.
The seas, mountains and animals are his.
He clothed all with his majesty.

Psalm 104:31 The glory of he Lord shall endure
for ever: the Lord shall rejoice in his works.

Appointed

Praise the God of Abraham, Isaac and Jacob.
His covenant commanded to a
thousand generations.
He protected and provided for his anointed.
Then and now he keeps those he appointed.

Psalm 105:4 Seek the Lord, and his
strength: seek his face evermore.

Ourselves

We have all sinned just as our forefathers,
Why do we turn away from what really matters?
Save us from ourselves O Lord!
Help us accept and live your words.

Psalm 106:3 Blessed are they that keep judgement,
and he that doeth righteousness at all times.

Releases

1. God has all power to build or destroy.
2. Do not tempt God!
3. Man is but a speck in time.
4. God created man.
5. Man tests and tempts God.
6. Despite his anger, God continues to forgive man.
7. One day God will release that anger.
8. Except for his mercy and love for man, we would not even be a memory.
9. Our call is to praise our God.
10. He has an inheritance with him for all who obey him and return his love.

Book 5

Wonder

Praise God for his goodness and wonders.
He soothes the storms of souls' longings.
Let his people thank him for his love.
He lifted the poor out of the dust.

Psalm 107:43 Whoso is wise, and will observe
these things, even they shall understand
the loving-kindness of the Lord.

Glory

I will awake early.
Sing a song of God's glory.
He will deliver us from enemies.
Honor him for future victories.

Psalm 108:4 For thy mercy is great above the
heavens: and thy truth reacheth unto the clouds.

Fall

First, I loved them and prayed for mercy.
Now they are wicked and lie against me.
Shame them Lord, let them fall.
Defend me. On you I call.

Psalm 109:4 For my love they are my
adversaries: but I give myself unto prayer.

Sit

Sit right by me and you will see.
I will bring down your enemies.
You, Lord are forever a priest.
You will judge and overthrow kings.

Psalm 110:5 The Lord at thy right hand shall
strike through kings in the day of his wrath.

Seek

Seek to work for the Lord.
His works are honorable and glorious.
God showed the people his power.
He set them free. Praise Him forever.

Psalm 111:10 The fear of the Lord
is the beginning of wisdom:

Delight

Fear the Lord and delight in his commandments.
Children of the upright, stay in remembrance.
Wealth, courage and compassion are the rewards.
They belong to the righteous that trust in the Lord.

Psalm 112:1 Praise ye the Lord. Blessed
is the man that feareth the Lord, that
delighteth greatly in his commandments.

Uplifting

Praise the name of the Lord.
He is now and forever more.
From on high He looks low.
He uplifts the poor and gives joy.

Psalm 113:4 The Lord is high above all
nations, and his glory above the heavens.

Sea

Great wonders our God did perform.
He delivered the Israelites across Jordon.
The sea parted at God's command.
He provided dry ground at his presence.

Psalm 114:7 Tremble, thou earth at the presence
of the Lord, at the presence of the God of Jacob;

Reward

Idols are deaf and dumb.
The same is true of them that trust in one.
Place all your hopes in the Lord.
He is the one who will bless and reward.

Psalm 115:11 Ye that fear the Lord, trust in
the Lord; he is their help and their shield.

Mercy

I was low, so close to death.
You lifted me and gave me health.
Your gracious mercy kept me living.
Now my vow to you, I am giving.

Psalm 116:18 I will pay my vows unto the
Lord now in the presence of all his people.

People

Praise the Lord every nation.
Praise him people from all stations!
He is merciful and He is kind.
His truth continues throughout time.

Psalm 117:1 O praise, the Lord...

Confidence

Put your faith in the Lord.
He is merciful and good.
Rejoice church in his strength.
In God, you can place your confidence.

Psalm 118:24 This is the day which the Lord
hath made: we will rejoice and be glad in it.

Doubt

When in doubt, turn to God.
Continue to read and trust his word.
Obey him. He will guide your feet,
He gives comfort, life and peace.

Psalm 119:105 Thy word is a lamp unto
my feet, and a light unto my path.

Distress

My soul is in distress.
God, to you I confess.
Deliver me from the guys,
Their deceitful tongues speak lies.

Psalm 120:2 Deliver my soul, O Lord from
lying lips, and from a deceitful tongue.

Preserves

Shall I be afraid of the hills today?
No. God will light my way.
At night also he keeps me.
He preserves my soul against evil.

Psalm 121:4 Behold, he that keepeth
Israel shall neither slumber nor sleep.

Abode

When invited, I was glad to go.
We are going into the Lord's abode!
Let us pray for peace to all.
May you be safe within those walls!

Psalm 122:2 Our feet shall stand
within thy gates, O Jerusalem.

Scorn

Lord, have mercy on our soul.
Some scorn what others hold.
My eyes look up to you, O God!
I wait for your approving nod.

Psalm 123:1 Unto thee lift I up mine eyes,
O thou that dwellest in the heavens.

Waters

The Lord was on our side!
We could have drowned in the tide!
Evil men fought against us.
We escaped from the waters!

Psalm 124:8 Our help is in the name of
the Lord, who made heaven and earth.

Anchor

Put your trust in the Lord.
He will be your anchor.
Stray from God's range.
You put yourself in danger.

Psalm 125:1 They that trust in the Lord
shall be as Mount Zion, which cannot
be removed, but abideth for ever.

Captivity

Find yourself when in captivity.
Cry unto the Lord for liberty.
God will turn your tears into joy.
He gives freedom, peace and love.

Psalm 126:3 The Lord, hath done great
things for us; whereof we are glad.

Rely

Guards, keep the Lord in your heart.
Laborers, give God his part.
Parents, raise your children right.
Everyone, rely on God for blessings in life.

Psalm 127:1 Except the Lord build the
house, they labor in vain that build it:

Follow

Fear the Lord.
Follow his laws.
You will be happy.
God blesses and gives peace.

Psalm 128:1 Blessed is everyone that feareth
the Lord; that walketh in his ways.

Stand

Time after time I was afflicted.
Again, my ruin they predicted.
The Lord saw and disapproved.
He cut them away.
I stand unmoved!

Psalm 129:4 The Lord is righteous: he hath cut asunder the cords of the wicked.

Forgiveness

When pressed down, I lifted my voice.
I prayed for forgiveness from my Lord!
In his word I place my hope.
I wait for redemption on my soul.

Psalm 130:7 Let Israel hope in the Lord:
for with the Lord there is mercy and
with him is plenteous redemption.

Behave

I am not proud.
I am not loud.
I behave myself.
All is done with God's help!

Psalm 131:3 Let Israel hope in the Lord
from henceforth and for ever.

Commit

I commit to the ark.
It is a place for my Lord!
Praise God for the covenant.
David's seed will rule and flourish.

Psalm 132:11 The Lord hath sworn in truth
unto David; he will not turn from it; of the
fruit of thy body will I set upon thy throne.

Anointed

Love God's people.
They live in peace.
All live as one.
Are they anointed?

Psalm 133:1 Behold, how good and how pleasant
it is for brethren to dwell together in unity.

House

Hands are raised tonight in God's house.
We send praises and announce.
Heaven and Earth the Lord installed!
His blessings, we applaud.

Psalm 134:2 Lift up your hands in the
sanctuary, and bless the Lord.

Name

Our Lord is great!
Praise his name!
Above him is no other!
His name endures forever!

Psalm 135:13 Thy name, O Lord,
endureth for ever; and thy memorial, O
Lord, throughout all generations.

Goodness

Give thanks to God's goodness.
We are born through his wisdom.
He alone delivered and kept us.
His mercy will live forever.

Psalm 136:26 O give thanks unto the God
of heaven: for his mercy endureth for ever.

Worth

How did you get your wealth?
Did you sacrifice people's health?
Is it worth all the hurt and pain?
We cannot sing a song in captivity!

Psalm 137:1 By the rivers of Babylon, there we sat down, yea, we wept, when we remembered Zion.

Trouble

With my whole heart I will praise.
I look to you, the God of my faith.
You send mercy when I am in trouble.
Forever your name deserves the glory.

Psalm 138:3 In the day when I cried
thou answeredst me, and strengthenedst
me with strength in my soul.

Eyes

It matters not where I go or what I do.
God is already there, he knows that too.
My creator is with me, and knows my cause.
There's no place to hide from the eyes of God!

Psalm 139:13 For thou, hast possessed my reigns…

Dwell

Preserve me Lord, O God of my strength.
Keep away the violent, lying evil men.
Turn their snares and words upon them.
Let only the righteous dwell in your presence.

Psalm 140:4 Keep me, O Lord, from the hands of
the wicked: preserve me from the violent man;

Guard

Hear me Lord I pray.
Guard my lips to what I say!
I do not want to be like my enemy.
Help me keep my words tasty.

Psalm 141:3 Set a watch, O Lord, before
my mouth; keep the door of my lips.

Overwhelmed

My spirit was overwhelmed.
My persecutors laid me a snare.
I cried out Lord, for you.
Help me and be my refuge!

Psalm 142:5 I cried unto thee O Lord:
I said Thou art my refuge and my
portion in the land of the living.

Justified

No living man can be justified.
All is guilty in the sight of our God.
We can only beg for his mercy.
He has to go in first place.

Psalm 143:9 Deliver me, O Lord, from mine
enemies: I flee unto thee to hide me.

Humbled

We thank you Lord, for strength and skills.
Give us victory if it is your will.
Your people are humbled by your greatness!
We'll sing to you new songs of praises.

Psalm 144:3 Lord, what is man, that thou
takest knowledge of him! or the son of
man, that thou makest account of him!

Generation

From one generation to the next,
Magnify God's name in speech and text.
Remember his acts, praise his name!
Our king provides; preserves and reigns.

Psalm 145:14 The Lord upholdeth all that fall,
and raiseth up all those that be bowed down.

Sing

Sing praises to God while alive.
He feeds the hungry, opens blind eyes.
Trust only in Him and you will see.
Our Creator will make you happy.

Psalm 146:5 Happy is he that hath
the God of Jacob for his help, whose
hope is in the Lord his God

Heart

The Lord heals the broken heart.
He blesses the offspring of Jacob.
Praise God, fear Him, and bless His name.
He fills with splendor and wonder, all he creates.

Psalm 147:5 Great is our Lord, and of great
power: his understanding is infinite.

Universal

Heavens hosts, praise the Lord!
Earth praises him, young and old.
Saints, God is merciful.
His power is universal!

Psalm 148:13 Let them praise the name of
the Lord: for his name alone is excellent;
his glory is above the earth and heaven

Kingdom

Rejoice Israel in your king.
Praise his name, dance and sing.
His kingdom has come.
Saints, take your vengeance.

Psalm 149:4 For the Lord taketh pleasure in his people: he will beautify the meek with salvation.

Breath

What are we called to do?
Who are we to give praises to?
Make music to God, for he is great!
Everything with breath, give God the praise!

Psalm 150:6 Let everything that
hath breath praise the Lord.

Rewinds

1. God knows your name.
2. God knows from where you came.
3. God desires man to worship him.
4. God is a creator – not a destroyer.
5. Man must look to God for solutions.
6. Man must suffer now to praise later.
7. God has your back if you are his saint.
8. Praise God always - in good times and bad.
9. Be humble. Fear and trust God.
10. God is great and good. Live and work for him. He has your best interest at heart.

Afterward

Our human existence is full of individual experiences that can cause us to soar high, glide to the side and/or sink deep. Praising God throughout all situations and looking to him for answers is the golden thread that runs through these poems, tying each back to the source. When you are angry, troubled, sick, doubtful, lonely, frustrated, abandoned and confused, reading this book can bring about joy, knowledge, fulfillment, peace, love, and spiritual riches through the acceptance of our Creator and fellowship with Him.

These poems are simple and powerful. They are inspired by God and as true today as they were yesterday. This is an easy read through which you can experience the protection and peace that comes with being close to God. If you have read Psalms, these poems help you reconnect and inspire you to read it once again.